1

Student's Book

58 St Aldates
Oxford
OX1 1ST
United Kingdom

Beep Student's Book / Activity Book Level 1

First Edition: 2014
ISBN: 978-607-06-0916-9

© Text: Brendan Dunne, Robin Newton
© Richmond Publishing, S.A. de C.V. 2014
Av. Río Mixcoac No. 274, Col. Acacias,
Del. Benito Juárez, C.P. 03240, México, D.F.

Publisher: Justine Piekarowicz
Editorial Team: Griselda Cacho, Rodrigo Caudillo, Diane Hermanson
Art and Design Coordinator: Marisela Pérez
Pre-Press Coordinator: Daniel Santillán

Illustrations: Gloria Celma, *Beehive Illustration*: Jim Peacock, Moreno Chiacchiera

Photographs: *A. Toril; C. Contreras; J. Jaime; M. Fernández; S. Enríquez;* A. G. E. FOTOSTOCK/SuperStock; ACI AGENCIA DE FOTOGRAFÍAAlamy Images; AGENCIA ESTUDIO SAN SIMÓN/ A. Prieto; COMSTOCK; CORDON PRESS/CORBIS/Beateworks/Fernando Bengoechea; GETTY IMAGES SALES SPAIN/ Photos.com Plus; HIGHRES PRESS STOCK/AbleStock.com; I. Preysler; ISTOCKPHOTO; Samsonite; MATTON-BILD; SERIDEC PHOTOIMAGENES CD/PHOTOALTO/Laurence Mouton; ARCHIVO SANTILLANA

Cover Design: Leandro Pauloni

All rights reserved. No part of this work may be reproduced, stored in a retrieval system or transmitted in any form or by any means without prior written permission from the Publisher.

Richmond publications may contain links to third party websites or apps. We have no control over the content of these websites or apps, which may change frequently, and we are not responsible for the content or the way it may be used with our materials. Teachers and students are advised to exercise discretion when accessing the links.

The Publisher has made every effort to trace the owner of copyright material; however, the Publisher will correct any involuntary omission at the earliest opportunity.

First published by Richmond Publishing / Santillana Educación S.L.

Printed in Brazil by Forma Certa Gráfica Digital
Lote: 796880
Cod: 292709169
2024

Contents

0 Hello!......2
1 At School......5
2 My Family......13
3 Perfect Pets......21

4 My Toys......29
5 In the House......37
6 My Body......45

7 My Favorite Food......53
8 At the Beach......61

Festivals......69

Hello!

LESSON 1

1 Listen and point.

2 Listen and chant.

LESSON 2

3 Look and trace.

4 Listen and point.

LESSON

5 Listen and sing.

One little, two little,
three little fingers,
Four little, five little,
six little fingers,
Seven little, eigth little,
nine little fingers,
Ten little fingers.

6 Listen, point and color.

1. At School

LESSON 1

1 Listen, point and repeat.

2 Listen, find and say. 1.1

LESSON 2

3 Listen and trace.

4 Listen, say and number. 1.2

LESSON 3

5 Trace and say.

1

2

glue

crayon

6 Listen and chant.

Hey, what's this?
Do you know?
It's a pen.
No, no, no!

Hey, what's this?
Can you guess?
It's a ruler.
Yes, yes, yes!

Let's Share!

LESSON

7 Listen to the story.

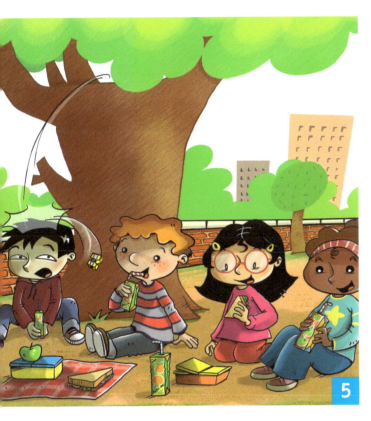 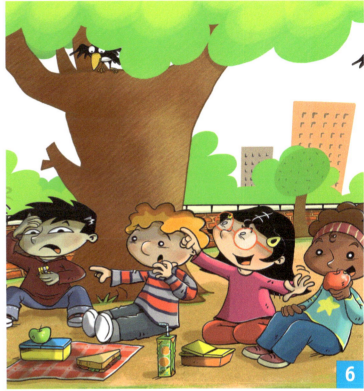

 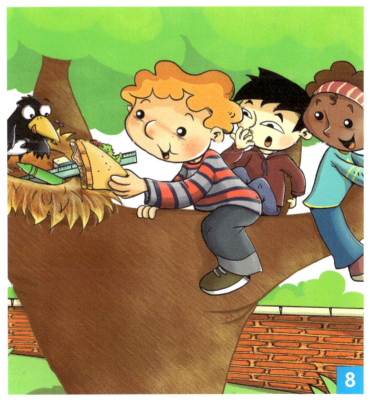

LESSON 5

8 Listen and stick.

1
Jim

2
Jenny

3
Lucy

9 Listen and sing.

Let's be friends,
Let's share our things,
Clap your hands and sing, sing, sing.

CLIL

LESSON 6

10 Look and say.

11 Read, stick and trace.

1 It's an eraser.

2 It's a crayon.

3 It's a pencil case.

11

PHONICS

Beep's World!

LESSON 7

12 Listen.

2. My Family

LESSON 1

1 Listen, point and repeat.

2 Listen and chant.

LESSON 2

3 Stick and trace.

"This is my family."

mom

grandpa

sister

dad

brother

grandma

4 Listen and point.

LESSON 3

5 Listen and sing.

This is my family.
Say "hello" to my family.
This is my family.

6 Look, stick and say.

grandpa

mom

Charlie

sister

15

The Surprise Party!

LESSON

7 Listen to the story.

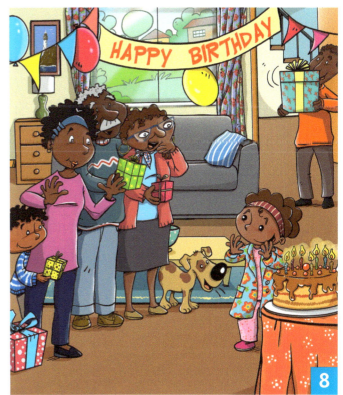

8 Listen, read and stick. 2.5

9 Listen and chant. 2.6

CLIL

LESSON 6

10 Trace and match.

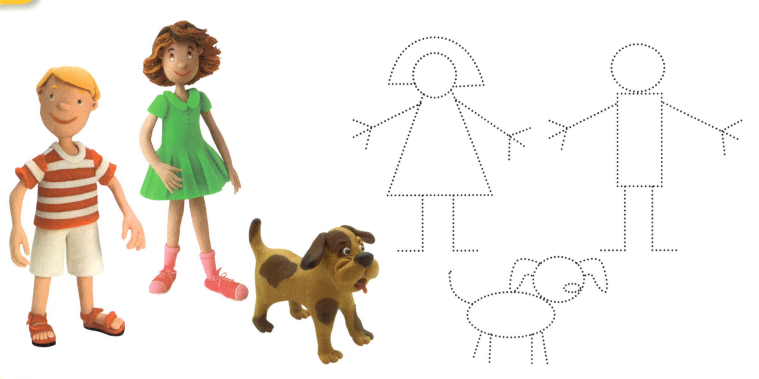

11 Look and draw.

19

Beep's World!

PHONICS

LESSON 7

12 Listen.

3. Perfect Pets

LESSON 1

1 Listen, point and repeat.

2 Listen and chant. 3.1

LESSON 2

3 Listen and circle.

1

2

3

4

4 Listen and sing.

Can you guess my pet?
Can you guess my pet?
Is it a hamster?
Is it a rabbit?
Can you guess my pet?

LESSON 3

5 Color and trace.

gray   brown   black   white

6 Stick and play.

Is it brown?

Yes, it is.
No, it isn't.

The Mystery of the Black Cat!

LESSON

7 Listen to the story.

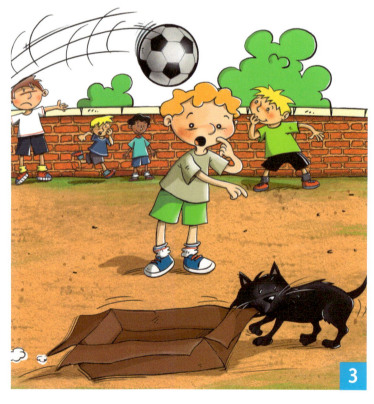

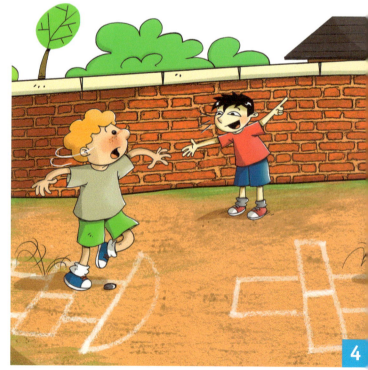

24

5

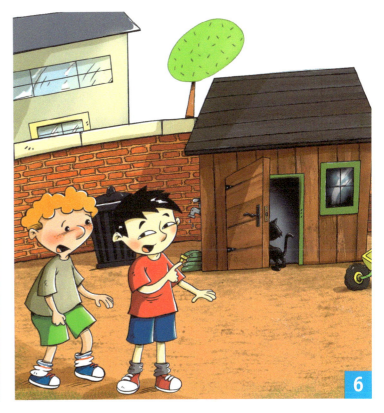

6

7

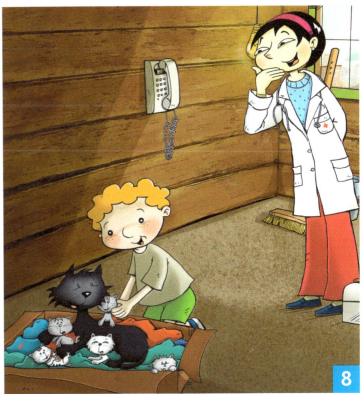

8

25

LESSON 5

8 Listen and point.

9 Listen and do.

CLIL

LESSON 6

10 Listen and number.

11 Draw your favorite pet.

My favorite pet is _____.

PHONICS

Beep's World!

LESSON 7

12 Listen.

28

4. My Toys

LESSON 1

1 Listen, point and repeat.

2 Listen and chant. 4.1

LESSON 2

3 Listen and check (✓) or cross (✗).

4 Ask and answer.

LESSON 3

5 Listen and chant.

Do you have a bike?
Do you have a bike?
Ruby, Ruby,
tell me please!
Yes, I do!

6 Ask and answer. Check (✓) or cross (✗).

Me

My friend

Computer Games Are Boring!

LESSON

7 Listen to the story.

LESSON 5

8 Play a game.

9 Listen and sing.

CLIL

LESSON 6

10 Listen and number.

11 Draw your favorite toy.

My favorite toy is a _____.

PHONICS

Beep's World!

LESSON 7

12 Listen. 🔊 4.7

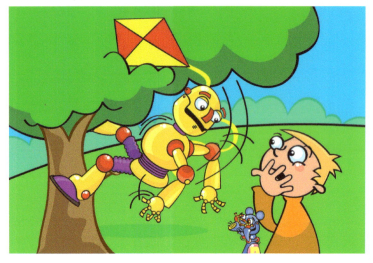

36

5. In the House

LESSON 1

1 Listen, point and repeat.

2 Listen and say the room. 5.1

LESSON 2

3 Listen and number.

4 Look and say.

LESSON 3

5 Listen and sing. 5.3

Where's my ruler?
Where's my ruler?
What can I do?
Look! It's in the kitchen!
Oh! Thank you!

6 Stick and say.

39

The Castle Adventure!

LESSON

7 Listen to the story.

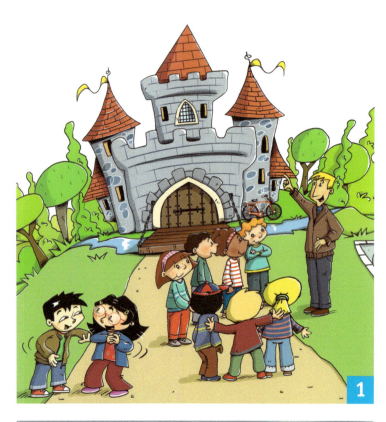
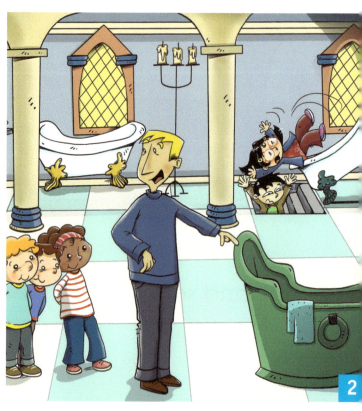
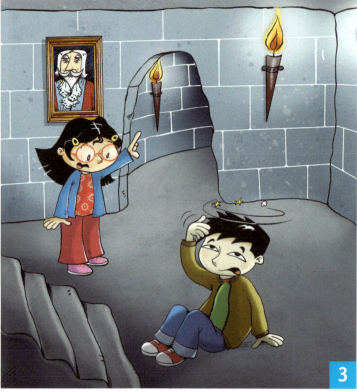
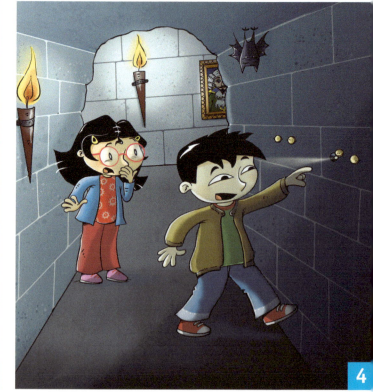

LESSON 5

8 Trace and stick.

9 Listen and point. 5.5

CLIL

LESSON 6

10 Listen and number.

11 Draw your favorite house.

My favorite house is a _____.

Beep's World!

PHONICS

LESSON 7

12 Listen. 5.7

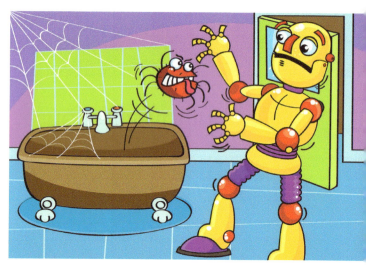

6. My Body

LESSON 1

1 Listen, point and repeat.

2 Listen and chant. 6.1

LESSON 2

3 Listen and stick.

4 Listen and chant.

All stand up and stamp your feet!
Move your body to the beat!
Wave your arms and touch your nose!
Shake your hands and touch your toes!

LESSON 3

5 Play a game.

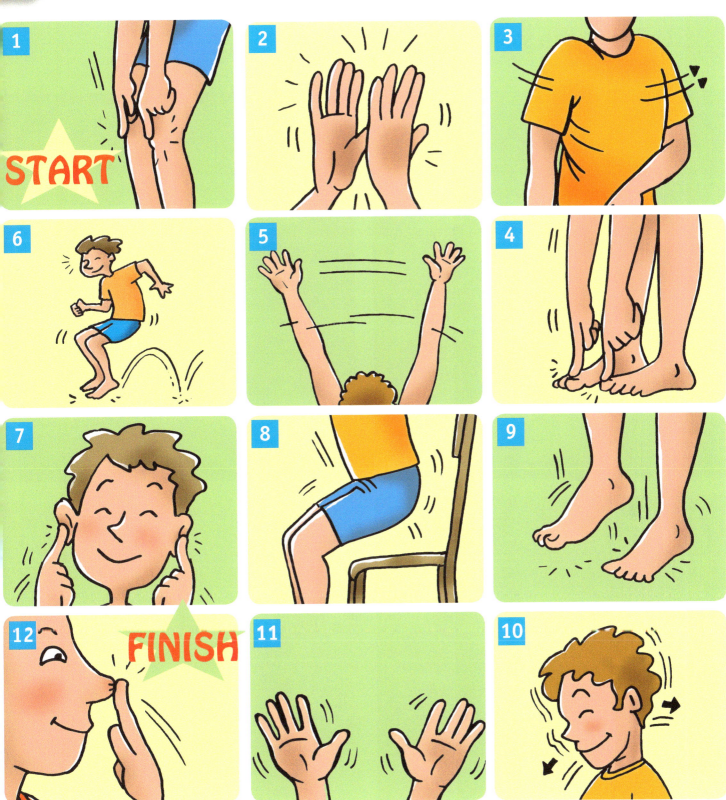

6 Look and say.

Charlie the Clown!

LESSON

 Listen to the story.

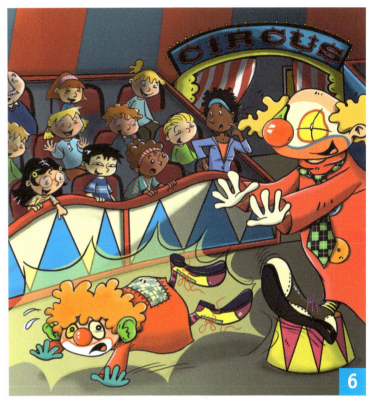

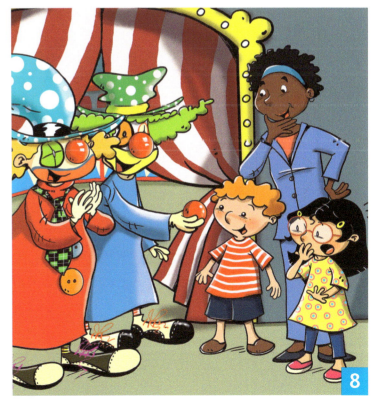

49

LESSON 5

8 Trace and say.

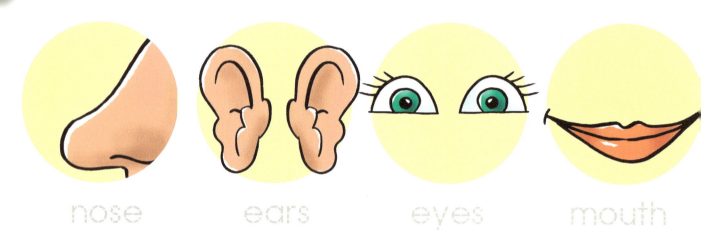

nose   ears   eyes   mouth

9 Listen and sing. 6.6

I'm Charlie the clown.
Stand up! Sit down!
I'm Charlie the clown.
Look at me!

PHONICS

Beep's World!

LESSON 7

12 Listen. 6.7

7. My Favorite Food

LESSON 1

1 Listen, point and repeat.

2 Listen and chant.

LESSON 2

3 Listen and draw. 7.2

4 Stick and say.

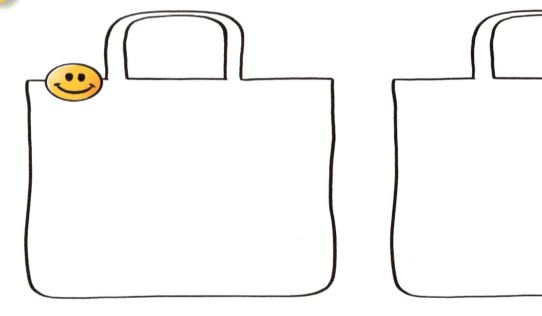

54

LESSON 3

5 Trace and say.

1. bread
2. milk
3. juice
4. hot dogs

6 Listen and sing.

I like oranges.
I like oranges.
Yes, I do. Yes, I do.
But I don't like apples.
No! No! No!
How about you?
How about you?

I like chocolate cake!

LESSON 4

7 Listen to the story.

LESSON 5

8 Trace, listen and check (✓) or cross (✗).

9 Ask and answer. Check (✓) or cross (✗).

58

CLIL

LESSON 6

10 Look and trace.

This pizza is from Italy.

This orange is from Spain.

This cake is from Germany.

This cheese is from France.

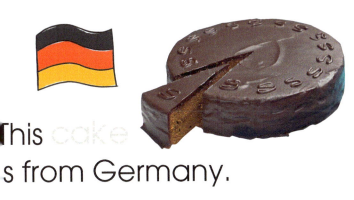

11 Draw your favorite food.

My favorite food is _____.

Beep's World!

PHONICS

LESSON 7

12 Listen. 7.6

60

8. At the Beach

LESSON 1

1 Listen, point and repeat.

2 Listen and chant. 8.1

LESSON 2

3 Listen and number.

4 Listen and sing.

At the beach,
At the beach.
What can you see?
Boys and girls and boats,
Boys and girls and boats.
That's what I can see.

LESSON 3

5 Listen and color.

6 Look and say.

What can you see?

63

A Day at the Amusement Park!

LESSON

7 Listen to the story.

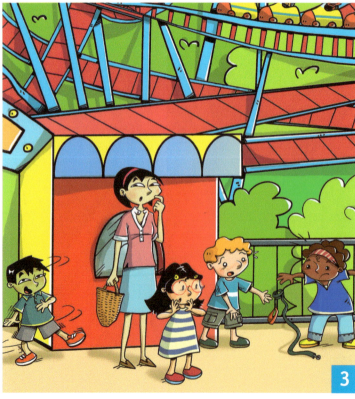

HOUSE OF MIRRORS

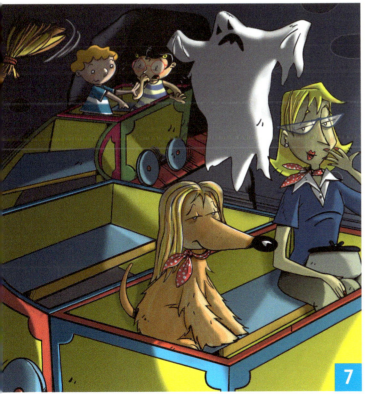

LESSON 5

8 Trace, listen and number.

I'm hungry!

I'm bored!

I'm scared!

I'm happy!

9 Listen and sing.

This is the way I eat a sandwich,
Eat a sandwich,
Eat a sandwich.
This is the way I eat a sandwich,
When I'm hungry.

CLIL

LESSON 6

10 Look and say.

11 Draw your own sand castle.

PHONICS

Beep's World!

LESSON 7

12 Listen. 8.7

68

Festivals

Halloween

1 Listen and point.

2 Listen and sing.

Halloween, Halloween.
What can you see?
I can see a scary ghost
chasing me.

Christmas

1 Color and say.

Christmas tree
star
reindeer
present
Santa

2 Listen and sing.

Here comes Santa.
Can you see?
Coming down the chimney,
With presents for you,
And presents for me!

Easter

1 Find and count.

☐ red eggs ☐ purple eggs ☐ yellow eggs
☐ green eggs ☐ blue eggs ☐ pink eggs

1 Match and say.

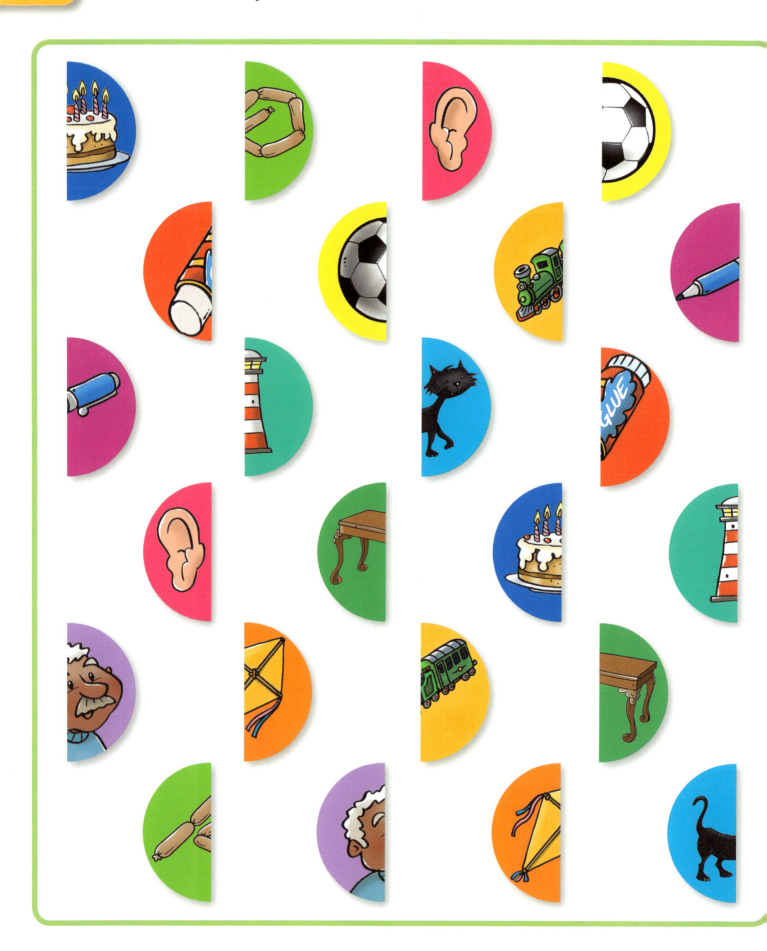

1

Activity Book

Richmond

Contents

0 Hello!......2

1 At School......3

2 My Family......5

3 Perfect Pets......7

4 My Toys......9

5 In the House......11

6 My Body......13

7 My Favorite Food......15

8 At the Beach......17

Festivals......19

Picture Dictionary......22

Track List......31

Hello!

1 Trace and match.

My name's Monica.
My name's Charlie.
My name's Lee.
My name's Ruby.

2 Draw and write.

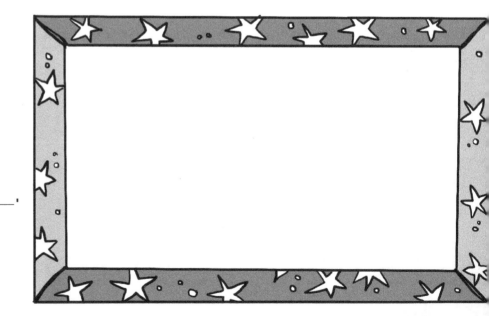

Hello! My name's

_____ .

1. At School

1 Find, circle and write.

1

glue

2

_____

r	u	l	e	r	t	p	o
s	r	e	z	i	a	h	x
p	e	n	t	b	o	o	k
z	p	e	n	c	i	l	e
e	r	a	s	e	r	o	b
m	a	c	r	a	y	o	n
g	l	u	e	t	i	p	u

3

_____

5

_____

4

_____

6

_____

7
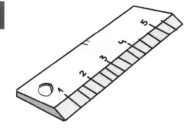
_____

2 Trace, match and color.

1 It's a pencil case.

2 It's a sharpener.

3 It's a pen.

4 It's a schoolbag.

5 It's a ruler.

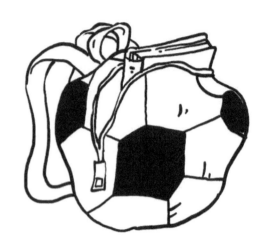

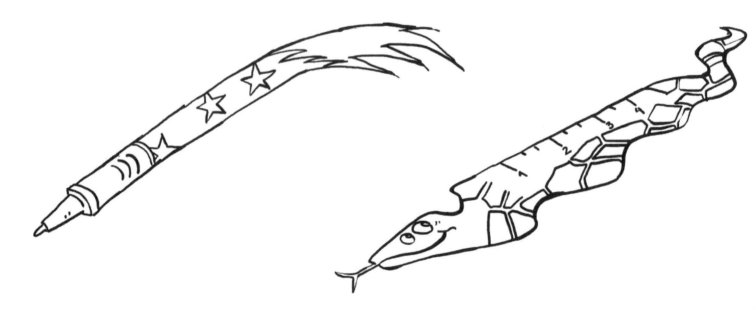

2. My Family

1 Read and match.

This is my brother.

This is my grandma.

This is my sister.

This is my dad.

2 Look and write.

I'm _____.

I'm _____.

I'm _____.

3 Match and color.

1 one   2 two   3 three   4 four   5 five

6 six   7 seven   8 eight   9 nine   10 ten

4 Trace, draw and write.

3. Perfect Pets

1 Read and color.

1 = black
2 = gray
3 = brown
4 = white

2 Look and write.

Yes, it is. ✓   No, it isn't. ✗

1  Is it a dog?

_____

2  Is it a rabbit?

_____

3 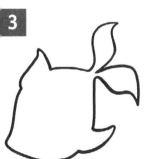 Is it a rat?

_____

4  Is it a frog?

_____

3 Trace and match.

4. My Toys

1 Look and write.

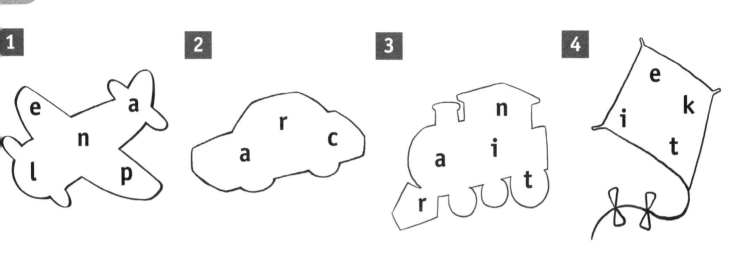

1. plane   2. car   3. train   4. kite

---

2 Read and write.

Do you have a train?   Do you have a ball?

3 Match and write.

car　　　train　　　kite　　　plane

I have a _____.

I have a _____.

I have a _____.

I have a _____.

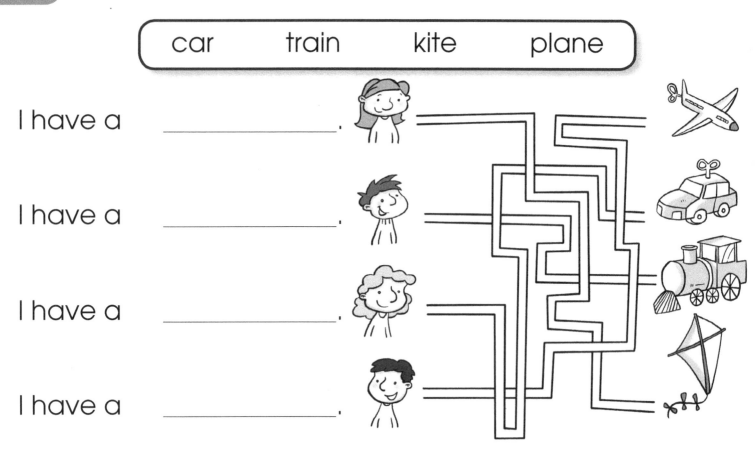

4 Read and color.

I have a yellow ball and a green plane.

I have a blue kite and a brown teddy bear.

I have a purple doll and a green train.

5. In the House

1 Look and write.

kitchen   bathroom   living room   bedroom

1. _____
2. _____
3. _____
4. _____

2 Write in or on.

1.  The book's __in__ the bag.

2.  The cat's _____ the table.

3.  The dog's _____ the chair.

4.  The teddy bear's _____ the bed.

11

3 Look and circle.

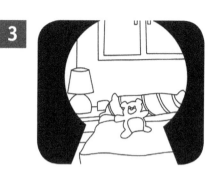

1 living room/hall   2 bathroom/garden   3 bedroom/kitchen

4 Draw  in the house and write.

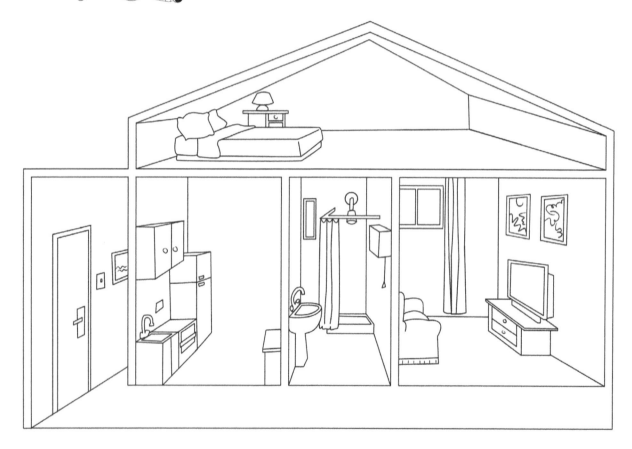

1 Where's the pencil? It's in the _____.

2 Where's the ball? _____.

3 Where's the car? _____.

12

6. My Body

1 Find and write.

1  eye

2

3

4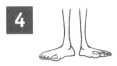

5

6

m	o	u	t	h	z	x	j	q
h	s	t	r	w	e	a	r	b
i	h	a	i	r	c	w	z	u
e	y	e	x	g	n	o	r	e
b	j	f	e	e	t	d	v	s
p	r	x	w	h	a	n	d	m

2 Write.

feet   arms   head   around

1  Nod your _____!

2 Stamp your _____!

3  Turn _____!

4  Wave your _____!

13

3 Trace and match.

1. stamp your feet
2. turn around
3. wave your arms
4. nod your head
5. shake your hands
6. touch your toes
7. clap your hands

4 Trace and number.

hair [2]
arm [ ]
hand [ ]
feet [ ]
leg [ ]
toes [ ]
knee [ ]
head [ ]

7. My Favorite Food

1 Circle and write.

bananajuicecheeseyogurtchickenapplemilkbread

2 Look and write.

☺ like   ☹ don't like

I _____ apples.   I _____ cheese.

3 Complete and circle.

apples   bread   juice   yogurt   ~~hot dogs~~   milk

Do you like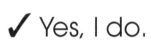
hot dogs ?

✓ Yes, I do.
✗ No, I don't.

Do you like
_____ ?

✓ Yes, I do.
✗ No, I don't.

Do you like
_____ ?

✓ Yes, I do.
✗ No, I don't.

Do you like
_____ ?

✓ Yes, I do.
✗ No, I don't.

Do you like
_____ ?

✓ Yes, I do.
✗ No, I don't.

Do you like
_____ ?

✓ Yes, I do.
✗ No, I don't.

8. At the Beach

1 Read, match and color.

boat   crab

shark   ocean

dolphin   lighthouse

seagull   sand castle

shell

2 Look and write.

I'm sad.   I'm hungry.   I'm scared.   I'm happy.

3 Trace and write check (✓) or cross (✗).

What can you see?

shark ✗
boat
sand castle
dolphin
crab
shell
lighthouse
seagull

4 Read and draw.

What can you see?

A blue lighthouse.

What can you see?

A yellow sand castle.

Festivals

Halloween

1 Trace and color.

2 Trace and number.

ghost

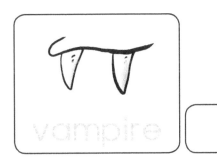
vampire

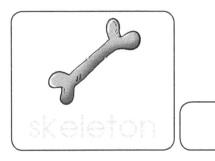
skeleton

witch

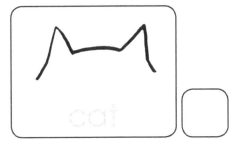
cat

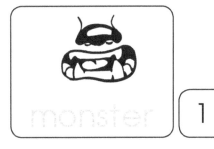
monster 1

Christmas

1 Read and color.

 star = yellow   Santa = red   present = orange
 Christmas tree = green   reindeer = brown

2 Draw your favorite present.

Easter

1 Read, match and color.

My egg's green.

My egg's red.

My egg's yellow.

My egg's purple.

My egg's pink.

21

Picture Dictionary 1

Picture Dictionary 2

brother

dad

grandma

grandpa

mom

sister

Picture Dictionary 3

cat
dog
frog

goldfish
hamster
parrot

rabbit
rat

Picture Dictionary 4

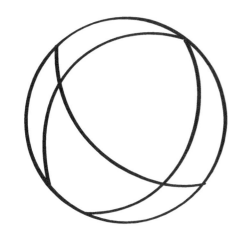

ball bike car

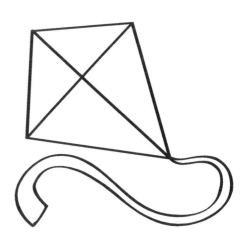

computer game doll kite

plane teddy bear train

Picture Dictionary 5

bathroom   bathtub   bed   bedroom

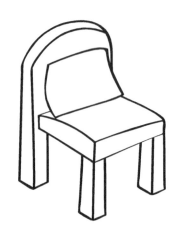  

chair   garden   hall

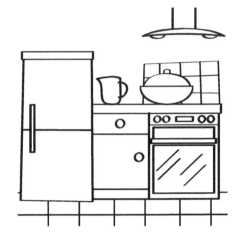  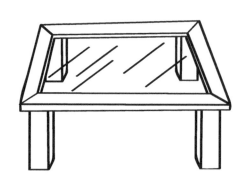

kitchen   living room   table

Picture Dictionary 6

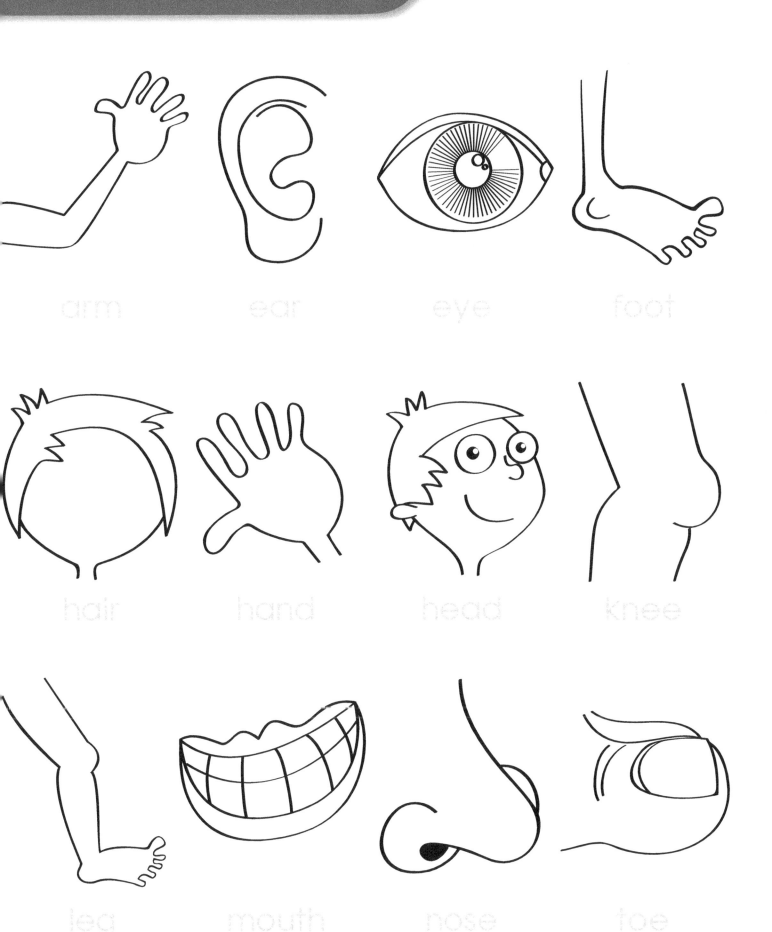

arm ear eye foot
hair hand head knee
leg mouth nose toe

Picture Dictionary 7

apple   banana   bread   cake

cheese   chicken   hot dog   juice

milk   orange   sandwich   yogurt

Picture Dictionary 8

boat　　　　　crab　　　　　dolphin

lighthouse　　　ocean　　　　sand castle

seagull　　　　shark　　　　shell

29

1 Draw and write.

LANGUAGE PASSPORT

Name: _____

Age: _____

Favorite toy: _____

Favorite pet: _____

Favorite food: _____

ABC123456-7

Me

Well Done! You have finished Beep Level 1. Now you can go on vacation!

LEVEL 2

Track List

Student's Book
Songs, chants and stories

Track	Transcript	
Unit 0		
1	0.2	Chant: Hey, hello!
2	0.4	Song: One, Two, Three Little Fingers!
Unit 1		
3	1.3	Chant: Hey, what's this?
4	1.4	Story: Let's share!
5	1.6	Song: Let's share!
6	1.7	Beep's World!
Unit 2		
7	2.1	Chant: The Family Chant
8	2.3	Song: This is my family.
9	2.4	Story: The Surprise Party!
10	2.6	Chant: How old are you?
11	2.7	Beep's World!
Unit 3		
12	3.1	Chant: The Pet Chant
13	3.3	Song: Can you guess my pet?
14	3.4	Story: The Mystery of the Black Cat!
15	3.7	Beep's World!
Unit 4		
16	4.1	Chant: The Toy Chant
17	4.3	Chant: Tell me, please!
18	4.4	Story: Computer games are boring!
19	4.5	Song: Toys, Toys, Toys!
20	4.7	Beep's World!
Unit 5		
21	5.3	Song: Ruby's Song
22	5.4	Story: The Castle Adventure!
23	5.7	Beep's World!
Unit 6		
24	6.1	Chant: I have hands and arms.
25	6.3	Chant: Stamp your feet!
26	6.4	Story: Charlie the Clown
27	6.6	Song: Charlie the Clown
28	6.7	Beep's World!

Track	Transcript	
Unit 7		
29	7.1	Chant: The Food Chant
30	7.3	Song: I like oranges.
31	7.4	Story: I like chocolate cake!
32	7.6	Beep's World!
Unit 8		
33	8.1	Chant: The Beach Chant
34	8.3	Song: At the Beach
35	8.4	Story: A Day at the Amusement Park!
36	8.6	Song: This Is the Way!
37	8.7	Beep's World!
Festivals		
38	F2	Song: The Halloween Song
39	F3	Song: The Santa Song

Activity Book
Picture Dictionary

Track	Transcript	
40	PD1	Picture Dictionary 1
41	PD2	Picture Dictionary 2
42	PD3	Picture Dictionary 3
43	PD4	Picture Dictionary 4
44	PD5	Picture Dictionary 5
45	PD6	Picture Dictionary 6
46	PD7	Picture Dictionary 7
47	PD8	Picture Dictionary 8